SUPER SAFETY HEROES

This book belongs to:

_____

ISBN: 978-1-952337-18-5

I'm a superhero. I tell folks every day,
"I don't need a cape to make a safer way."

People giggle at me. They think that I'm too young
to care about emergencies but safety's lots of fun!

I tell them, "Safety is important. Safety can be cool.
Safety is for everyone so pack up all your tools!"

I'm a superhero, I tell folks every day,
"Listen up and pay attention, safety is the way."

We can all pack a safety kit and it can save a life.

We can create safety plans and practice until it's right.

We can be whistleblowers if we need a crisis noise.

We can use the phone, call for help and use a brave voice.

You're a superhero. I tell folks every day,
"You don't need a cape to make a safer way."

People giggle at me, they think that I'm too young to care
but I made a safety flyer for everyone to share.

It read, "Superhero Party: Be There If You're Cool!
Come share your awesome powers and bring a safety tool."

I cranked up the music and made some yummy treats.

I drew a welcome sign and poured up punch bowl drinks.

I taped up bright streamers and blew up big balloons.

The doorbell rang and then I heard a loud familiar tune.

"We are superheroes. We tell folks every day.
We don't need a cape to make a safer way!"

We all giggled and we boogied. Everyone was there.
We shared our safety tips with superhero safety care!

Safety Signs

Be aware & use your mind,
can you identify these important safety signs?

Empower yourself.

Safety Word Search

Be alert & look alive!
Find the words
for safety time...

B	A	G	R	N	O	I	T	U	A	C	R	D	X	C
I	S	R	I	H	G	F	H	X	I	M	L	F	T	A
B	S	Y	B	C	E	L	R	S	G	W	J	M	V	R
V	O	E	M	H	Q	R	R	N	I	J	A	P	C	E
L	G	S	I	F	C	T	O	A	S	X	C	T	S	F
Q	E	F	B	E	O	R	L	L	Z	B	E	E	E	X
P	H	L	W	Y	M	S	U	P	P	L	I	E	S	R
N	H	A	Z	A	R	D	N	U	S	R	A	H	J	R
E	L	S	I	X	A	Z	Y	E	E	Y	M	V	H	T
G	P	H	G	E	A	V	H	T	H	P	H	J	E	O
H	S	L	D	N	F	P	T	V	T	G	A	J	L	S
W	O	I	B	H	Q	A	I	B	O	A	C	M	P	C
U	N	G	H	F	B	F	M	Y	L	B	M	N	M	O
J	W	H	S	A	O	V	O	Y	C	Y	V	L	T	N
N	H	T	X	I	D	O	U	L	Z	T	A	N	K	T
F	I	R	S	T	A	I	D	I	O	E	W	W	E	A
T	S	J	K	V	N	B	H	K	P	F	T	D	V	C
A	T	T	A	S	G	Z	A	K	Q	A	Q	K	A	T
F	L	P	R	W	E	V	A	E	J	S	X	R	R	S
R	E	W	A	K	R	L	Y	O	X	E	Q	X	B	L

BATTERIES
BRAVE
CARE
CAUTION
CLOTHES
CONTACTS
DANGER
FIRSTAID
FLASHLIGHT
FOOD
HAZARD
HELP
HERO
PLANS
SAFETYBAG
SUPPLIES
WATER
WHISTLE

Believe in yourself.

Safety Bag Checklist

If you're ever in a crisis there are great items to have,
do your best to put together your own safety bag!

Here's a great start:

- ☐ FIRST AID KIT
- ☐ EMERGENCY CONTACTS
- ☐ WATER
- ☐ DRY SNACKS
- ☐ FLASHLIGHT
- ☐ EXTRA BATTERIES
- ☐ WHISTLE
- ☐ HAND SANITIZER
- ☐ SHIRT
- ☐ PANTS

- ☐ SOCKS
- ☐ BLANKET
- ☐ TOWEL
- ☐ FACE MASK
- ☐ PLASTIC GLOVES
- ☐ PAPER TOWELS
- ☐ SOAP
- ☐ TOOTH BRUSH
- ☐ TOOTH PASTE
- ☐ TEDDY BEAR

SAFETY

stay prepared.

Emergency Contact List

Write the names and phone numbers of trusted people in one place.
Call them if you're in a crisis or if you don't feel safe.

SAFE PERSON #1

NAME:_____

PHONE NUMBER: _____

THIS PERSON IS A TRUSTED :

- ☐ FAMILY MEMBER
- ☐ FRIEND
- ☐ COMMUNITY MEMBER

SAFE PERSON #2

NAME:_____

PHONE NUMBER: _____

THIS PERSON IS A TRUSTED :

- ☐ FAMILY MEMBER
- ☐ FRIEND
- ☐ COMMUNITY MEMBER

SAFE PERSON #3

NAME:_____

PHONE NUMBER: _____

THIS PERSON IS A TRUSTED :

- ☐ FAMILY MEMBER
- ☐ FRIEND
- ☐ COMMUNITY MEMBER

Stay connected.

Special Information

Fill out your special information, if you need help ask a safe person to assist you. If you're ever in an emergency, this information can be helpful to you.

MY NAME IS _____.

I'M A SUPER SAFETY HERO AND I AM _____ YEARS OLD.

MY CAREGIVER'S NAME IS _____.

MY BIRTHDAY IS ON _____.

MY FAVORITE THINGS ARE _____

_____.

I FEEL SAFE WHEN _____

_____.

MY SPECIAL NEEDS ARE _____

_____

_____

_____

_____

you are important.